WHAT'S OLDER THAN A GIANT TORTOISE?

Robert E. Wells

Albert Whitman & Company · Morton Grove, Illinois

For my stepson, Kurt, daughter-in-law, Vira, and my grandchildren, Joanna and Jason. May your adventuresome spirit continue . . .

Library of Congress Cataloging-in-Publication Data

Wells, Robert E.
What's older than a giant tortoise? / written and illustrated by Robert E. Wells.
p.   cm.
ISBN 0-8075-8831-8 (hardcover)
ISBN 0-8075-8832-6 (pbk.)
1. Science—Miscellanea—Juvenile literature. I. Title.
Q163.W427   2004
500—dc22   2004000868

Hand-lettering by Robert E. Wells.
The illustration media are pen and acrylic.
Design by Susan B. Cohn.

Also by Robert E. Wells
Can You Count to a Googol?
How Do You Know What Time It Is?
How Do You Lift a Lion?
Is a Blue Whale the Biggest Thing There Is?
What's Faster Than a Speeding Cheetah?
What's Smaller Than a Pygmy Shrew?

If medals were given to animals for living a very long time, a GIANT TORTOISE would win one for sure.

VERY-LONG-LIVING ANIMAL
AWARD
WINNER

GIANT TORTOISE
AGE: 150 years
LENGTH: 5 feet
WEIGHT: 500 lbs.

Some giant tortoises live more than 150 years—longer than any other known land animal.

Most giant tortoises live in the Galápagos Islands, near Ecuador, or on Aldabra Island, just north of Madagascar.

If *you* were a 150-year-old giant tortoise who'd just won a medal for living a very long time, you might feel quite proud.

This GIANT SEQUOIA TREE is *much* older than you.

Giant sequoias grow on the western slopes of the Sierra Nevada in California.

They are one of the oldest and biggest living things on Earth.

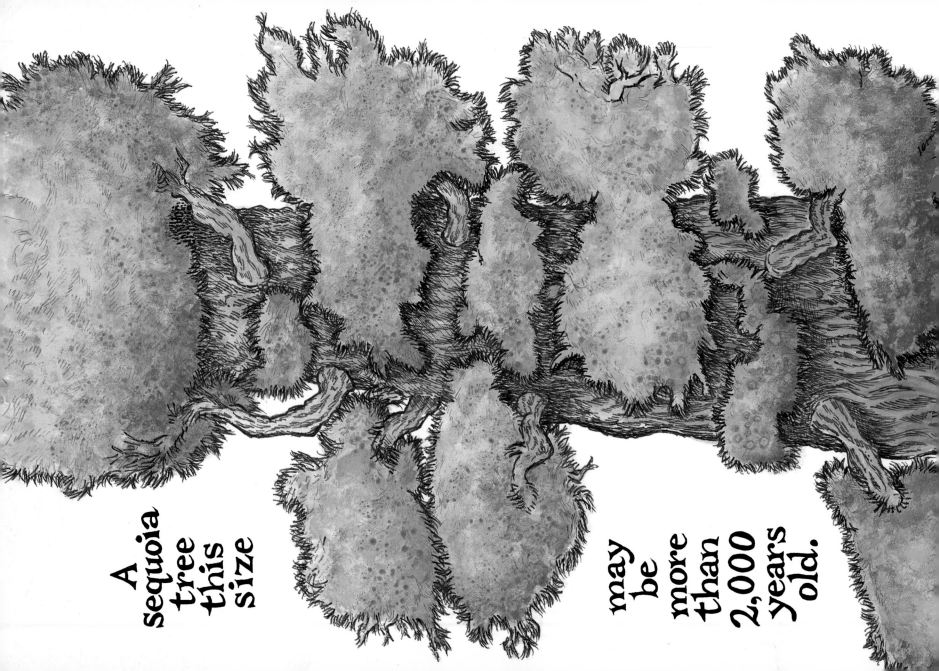

A sequoia tree this size

may be more than 2,000 years old.

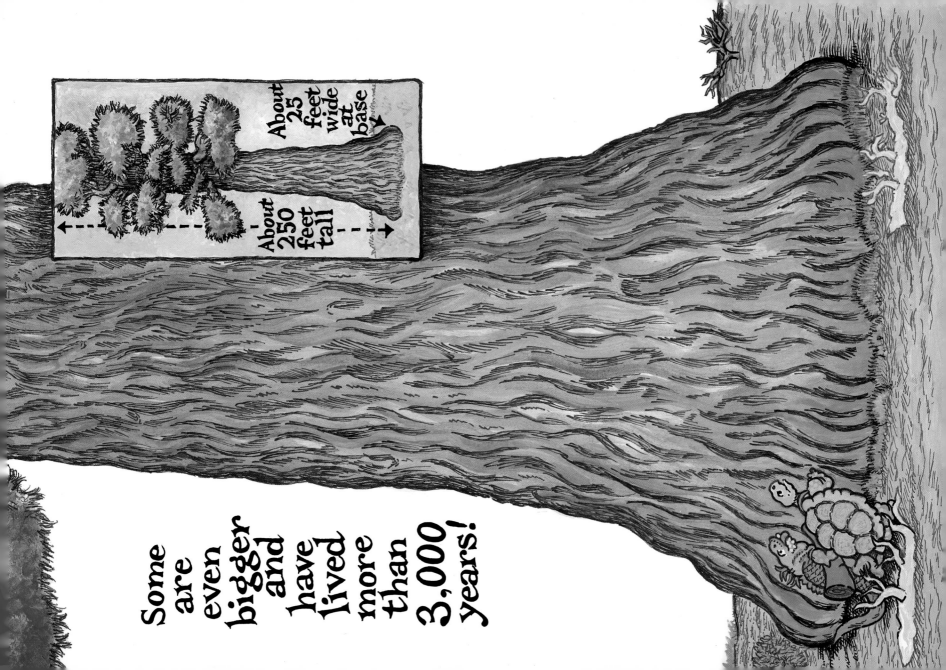

About 25 feet wide at base

About 250 feet tall

Some are even bigger and have lived more than 3,000 years!

CROSS SECTION of a GIANT SEQUOIA TREE

By counting the rings on the cross section of a tree, you are counting the years it lived.

But it would sure be easy to lose count on a very old tree!

Yes, a giant sequoia tree can be mighty old. But not as old as...

the PYRAMIDS of GIZA, in Egypt. They were built by the Egyptians about 4,500 years ago, as tombs for Egyptian rulers, called pharaohs.

Egypt's pyramids are among the world's oldest structures made by people.

But if you look in the right place, you'll see something even *older*—made by an invader from outer space!

This is METEOR CRATER, in Arizona. The "invader from outer space" that made this crater was a meteor about 150 feet wide.

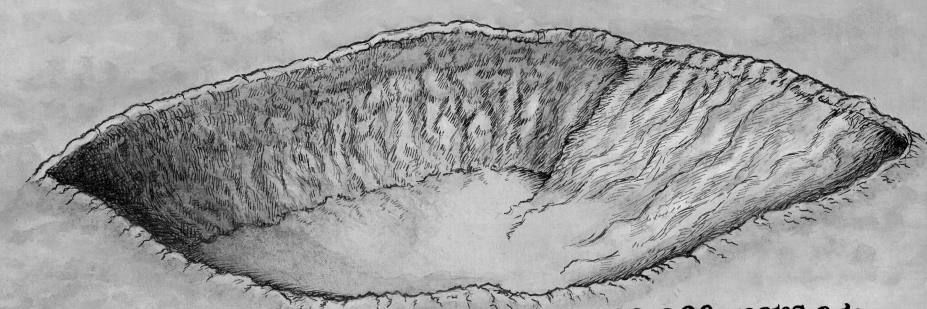

It collided with Earth about 49,000 years ago, traveling at 40,000 miles per hour!

Meteor Crater is just one of more than 160 impact craters that have been discovered on Earth.

(1) METEOR SPEEDS TOWARD EARTH.

(2) METEOR'S IMPACT BLASTS EARTH MATERIAL AWAY,

(3) MAKING A CRATER MUCH BIGGER THAN THE METEOR.

It's about ¾ mile wide, and about 560 feet deep!

Meteor Crater is more than 10 times older than Egypt's pyramids...

but many MAMMOTH FOSSILS are even older.

Bone fossils are the remains of animals that lived thousands—or even millions—of years ago.

MAMMOTH RECONSTRUCTION

MAMMOTH FOSSIL SITE

EXCAVATION IN PROGRESS

OUT to LUNCH

Scientists called paleontologists have found fossils of many extinct animals, including mammoths.

as MOUNT EVEREST, the world's highest mountain. Mount Everest is about $5\frac{1}{2}$ miles high. It's part of Asia's Himalayan mountain range.

The Himalayas began to form millions of years ago, when the landmasses of India and Asia, which were then separate,

began pushing together, causing the land between to crumple.

DIRECTION OF PUSH →

OCEAN WATER BETWEEN LAND PUSHED AWAY ↓

INDIA

ASIA

HIMALAYAS BEGIN TO RISE WHEN LANDMASSES PUSH TOGETHER ↴

INDIA

ASIA

Mount
Everest rose
to its great
height about
17 million
years ago.

But, giant tortoise,
you can see things
even older than Mount
Everest, if you know
just where to look.

In New York City's American Museum of Natural History, you can see a fossil skeleton of a TYRANNOSAURUS REX, or T. rex, who lived about 65 million years ago.

Tyrannosaurus rex

HEIGHT: about 15 feet

LENGTH: about 40 feet

The Age of Dinosaurs began about 225 million years ago, and ended about 65 million years ago, when the last dinosaurs mysteriously died out.

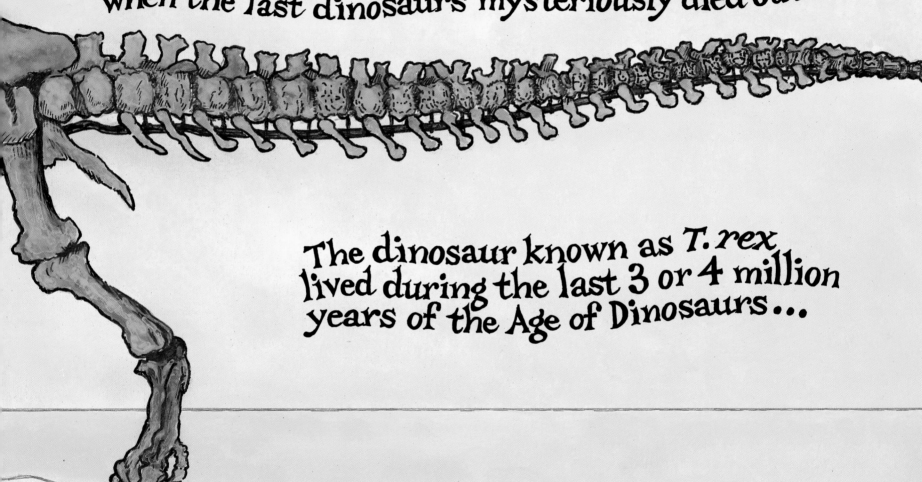

The dinosaur known as *T. rex* lived during the last 3 or 4 million years of the Age of Dinosaurs...

and was surely one of the most ferocious-looking creatures that ever lived!

Now hold your breath
and hang on tight.

To get a better view of
some older things, it'll take
a higher carpet ride.

From up here in space, you can see our whole planet EARTH. It's about 4.6 billion years old. Our MOON is about the same age.

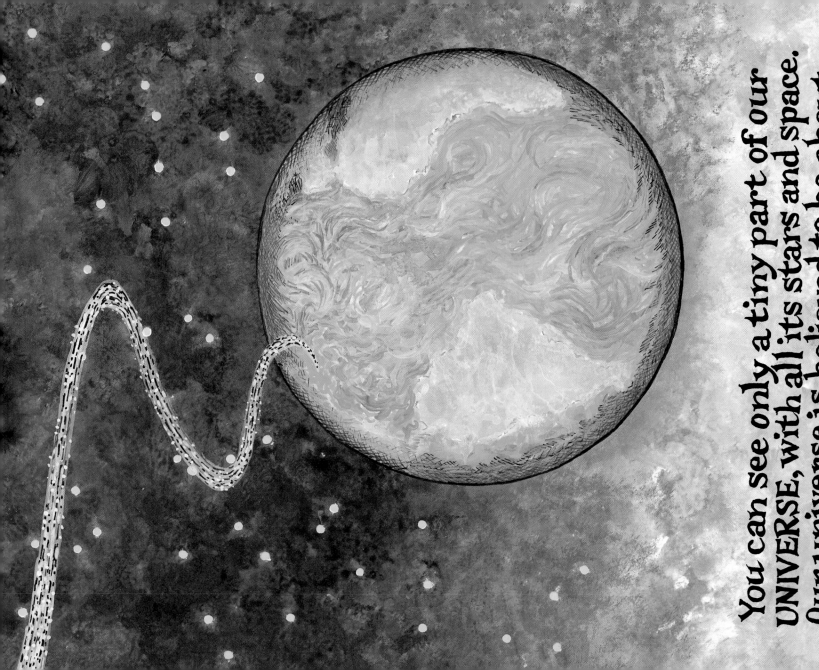

You can see only a tiny part of our UNIVERSE, with all its stars and space. Our universe is believed to be about 13.7 billion years old.

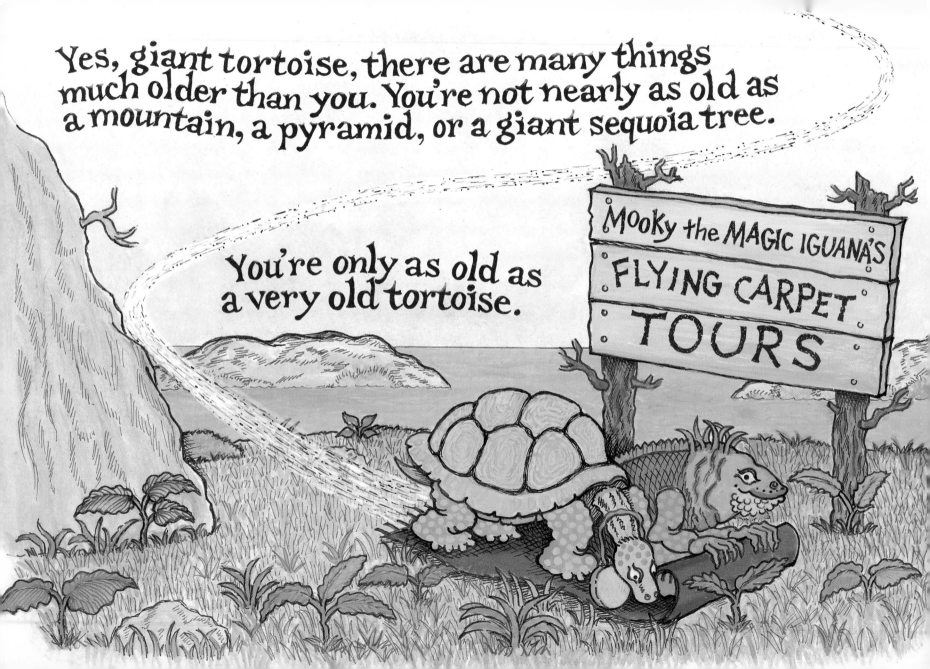

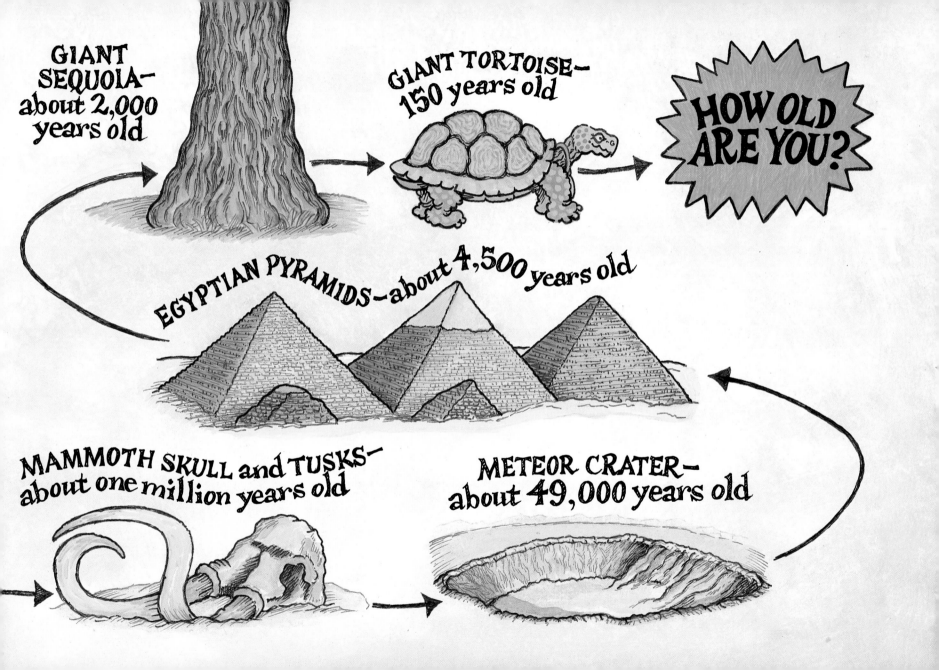

GIANT SEQUOIA— about 2,000 years old

GIANT TORTOISE— 150 years old

HOW OLD ARE YOU?

EGYPTIAN PYRAMIDS— about 4,500 years old

MAMMOTH SKULL and TUSKS— about one million years old

METEOR CRATER— about 49,000 years old

If you looked into the wrinkled eyes of an old giant tortoise, you might sense he'd lived a very long time—and you'd surely be right. Written records show that giant tortoises can live more than 150 years.

A tree's age is recorded in growth rings, and the ages of Egypt's pyramids are recorded in written history. To find the age of older things, like fossils and mountains, scientists use RADIOMETRIC DATING.

Radiometric dating uses our knowledge of how atoms behave. Certain kinds of atoms change into other atoms over a long period of time. By measuring the number of atoms that have changed in a fossil or a rock, scientists are able to make an accurate estimate of how old the fossil or rock is. Using radiometric dating, they have made a close estimate of the age of the planet Earth—about 4.6 billion years.

The Hubble Space Telescope, launched in 1990, has helped astronomers figure out the universe's approximate age. But by measuring the temperature of cosmic radiation with a new space probe launched in 2001, astronomers were able to make an even closer estimate of the age of the universe—about 13.7 billion years old.